David Ortiz

By Jeff Savage

AMAZING ATHLETES

Lerner Publications Company • Minneapolis

For Bailey Savage, my power-hitting son

Lerner Publications Company
A division of Lerner Publishing Group
241 First Avenue North
Minneapolis, MN 55401 U.S.A.

Website address: www.lernerbooks.com

Library of Congress Cataloging-in-Publication Data

Savage, Jeff, 1961–
    David Ortiz / by Jeff Savage.
        p.   cm. — (Amazing athletes)
    Includes index.
    ISBN-13: 978-0-8225-3429-7 (lib. bdg. : alk. paper)
    ISBN-10: 0-8225-3429-0 (lib. bdg. : alk. paper)
    1. Ortiz, David, 1975– —Juvenile literature. 2. Baseball players—Dominican Republic—Biography—Juvenile literature. I. Title. II. Series.
GV865.O78S28 2006
796.357'092—dc22   2005020826

Manufactured in the United States of America
  2 3 4 5 6 – DP – 11 10 09 08 07 06

Table of Contents

David's great hitting has made him one of baseball's most popular players.

A HERO IS BORN

David Ortiz's team needed help. David's Boston
Red Sox were playing the New York Yankees in
the 2004 American League Championship

Series (ALCS). The Red Sox had lost the first three games of the series. If David's team lost one more game, their season would be over. The Yankees would go on to the **World Series.**
But David and his teammates would not give up. The Red Sox battled the Yankees all night. They took a 4–4 tie into **extra innings.** In the 12th inning, the Red Sox got a runner on base. Then David came to bat. Red Sox fans screamed, "Papi! Papi!" Big Papi is David's nickname.

David takes a big swing at a pitch.

Yankees pitcher Paul Quantrill fired a pitch over the plate. David swung hard. *Crack!* The baseball soared high into the night sky. It sailed over the right field wall for a **home run.** The crowd roared. The Red Sox had won the game, 6–4!

"We're still alive!" David told reporters in the locker room. He flashed his wide smile.

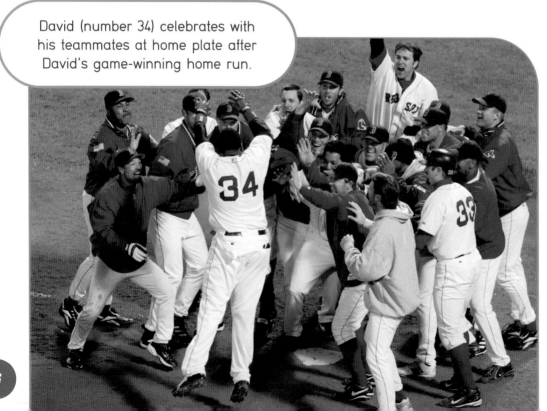

David (number 34) celebrates with his teammates at home plate after David's game-winning home run.

Yankees pitcher Mariano Rivera
is one of the best pitchers David
has ever faced.

But the Red Sox had to win three more games to get to the World Series. Game 5 was played the next night. By the eighth inning, the Red Sox were in trouble again. David's team was losing 4–2. They faced one of baseball's toughest pitchers, Mariano Rivera. David stepped up to the plate. He swung hard at a Rivera pitch.

David watches as the ball he hit sails into center field for a game-winning hit.

Thwack! The ball sailed deep to left. It flew over the left field wall for a home run. Then the Red Sox scored another run to tie the game, 4–4.

The teams battled into extra innings again. In the 14th inning, Red Sox center fielder Johnny Damon got on base. Once again, David came up to bat. The crowd stood and chanted. Yankees pitcher Esteban Loiaza threw a pitch. *Crack!* David smashed the ball into center field for a base hit. Damon crossed home plate with the winning run. David Ortiz had struck again!

Young boys play baseball in the Dominican Republic. Many Dominican kids grow up hoping to become Major League Baseball stars like David Ortiz.

GROWING UP HAPPY

David Américo Ortiz Arias was born November 18, 1975. His father's name is Américo. His mother's name was Angela Rosa Arias. David used the last name Arias until he was an adult.

David's hero growing up was comic book superhero Captain America.

David and his family grew up in the Dominican Republic. This country is part of a large island southeast of Florida in the Caribbean Sea. David's family lived in the country's capital, Santo Domingo.

David was a happy boy. He liked to laugh and joke around with his friends. He also liked to play sports. Baseball, basketball, and soccer were his favorites.

David grew up to be a big, strong kid. He was one of the best athletes in his neighborhood. David's best sport was baseball. He was a super hitter. He could smack the ball a long way.

Baseball is the most popular sport in the Dominican Republic. Children play the game on dirt fields. But many Dominican kids are too poor to buy bats and balls. So they use wooden sticks for bats and oranges for balls.

David was also a good basketball player. He was the best player on his team at Estudia Espallat High School. By this time, David was six feet four inches tall. He was so big and strong that most kids could not stop him from scoring baskets. David hoped he could become a pro athlete in one of his two favorite sports.

David is just one of many great baseball players from the Dominican Republic. David's teammate Manny Ramirez is Dominican. Others include Vladimir Guerrero of the Los Angeles Angels of Anaheim, Albert Pujols of the St. Louis Cardinals, and Miguel Tejada of the Baltimore Orioles.

David practices at first base while playing for the Wisconsin Timber Rattlers.

MAKING THE BIG LEAGUES

David wasn't quite good enough to become a
pro basketball player. But he had all the skills to
be a great baseball hitter. He had quick hands.
They helped him swing the bat fast enough to

hit fast pitches. And he was very strong. This helped him to hit the ball a long way.

Scouts for Major League Baseball teams watched David play in high school. They saw him hit long home runs. The Seattle Mariners liked David's skills. In 1992, the Mariners offered David a contract. He signed on to play for a Mariners team in the minor leagues. David had just turned 17 years old. He would have to work his way up to the major leagues.

Early in 1994, David moved to the United States. He joined a Mariner minor league team in Arizona. He enjoyed two great seasons. In 1996, the Mariners sent David to play for their minor league team in Appleton, Wisconsin. Playing for the Wisconsin Timber Rattlers, he hit 34 doubles. He had a high batting average of .322 and smacked 18 home runs.

David and his wife, Tiffany, met when David was playing for the Timber Rattlers.

The Mariners traded David to the Minnesota Twins before the 1997 season. Around the same time, David dropped "Arias" from his name. He asked people to call him David Ortiz.

David had a huge year in 1997. He had a batting average over .300. In September, the Twins called him up to the major league team. In his second game for the Twins, David smacked a double for his first major league hit. A week later, he blasted his first home run. When the season ended, David had high hopes. He wanted to be the Twins' starting first baseman in 1998.

David congratulates his teammate Jacque Jones after Jones hit a home run.

HARD TIMES

The 1998 season started out great for David. He began with a seven-game **hitting streak.** But then, he broke his wrist. He couldn't play for almost two months. But he played well when he returned to the Twins.

David's career with the Twins had many ups and downs.

David hoped to keep up his hot hitting in 1999. But he started out poorly in **spring training.** So the Twins sent him back to the minor leagues.

Playing for the Salt Lake Stingers, he cracked 30 home runs. He also led the league in **runs batted in.** But the Twins didn't call him up to the major leagues. He had to wait to get another chance.

David returned to the Twins in 2000. But playing for the Twins wasn't always fun. They were a losing team. They lost 93 games and won only 69.

David had some bad times with the Twins, but he kept smiling. He kept his good sense of humor. He was always telling jokes and making his teammates laugh. David was a very popular player. His teammates liked him, and Twins fans liked him.

David walks back to the dugout with his teammate Bobby Kielty after Kielty hit a home run.

But things kept going wrong in Minnesota. In 2001, David broke his wrist again. He missed a lot of games. When he got back, he struggled. David finished the year with a low .234 batting average.

But the biggest disaster hit David after the season. His mother was killed in a car accident. David was heartbroken. To remember her, he wears a big tattoo of her on his arm.

David proudly shows off the tattoo of his mother.

The Twins turned things around in 2002. David hit 20 home runs, and the Twins won 94 games. The team made it to the **playoffs** for the first time in years. Minnesota beat the Oakland A's in an exciting American League **Division Series.** Then they lost to the Anaheim Angels in the ALCS. It had been a fun year. But David wasn't sure he would be back with the Twins in 2003.

After losing a playoff game, David sits quietly in the dugout. The 2002 playoffs would be the last games David played for the Twins.

David and his teammate Manny Ramirez (left) were the two best hitters in a powerful Red Sox lineup.

WINNING IT ALL

The Twins needed to save money on player salaries. So they let David become a **free agent.** Any team could take him. The Boston Red Sox signed him to a one-year contract for more than $1 million. David was thrilled to get a fresh start.

The Red Sox made David their **designated hitter.** Red Sox batting coach Ron Jackson helped David with his hitting. David bashed an amazing 31 homers in 2003. The Red Sox won 95 games and made the playoffs.

David hit a game-winning double to beat the Oakland A's in the Division Series. The Red Sox went on to face the New York Yankees in the American League Championship Series. The two teams battled for seven exciting games. In Game 7, David hit a home run to give the Red Sox the lead. But the Yankees came back and won the game.

David and his wife, Tiffany, have a home near Green Bay, Wisconsin. They live there with their daughters, Jessica and Alexandra, and son, D'Angelo.

Red Sox players and fans were crushed. They had come so close to getting to the World Series! But David promised to keep trying. "I love Boston," David said. "I want to bring the fans a World Series title."

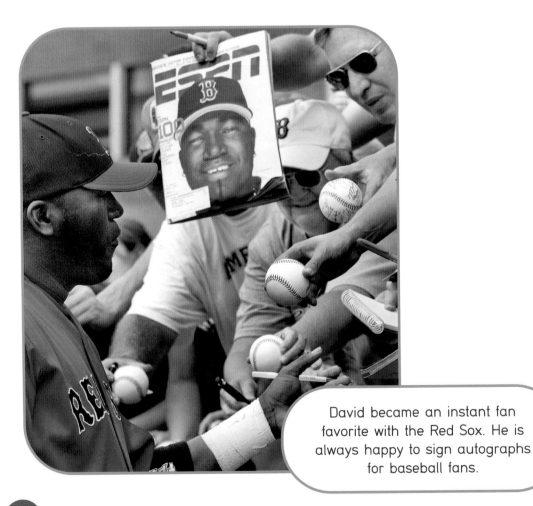

David became an instant fan favorite with the Red Sox. He is always happy to sign autographs for baseball fans.

David smacks a hit to left field.

The Red Sox knew they had a star in David Ortiz. Before the 2004 season, they signed him to a two-year contract for more than $12 million. They also brought in superstar pitcher Curt Schilling. The Red Sox had one of their best teams ever.

David had a monster season in 2004. He batted .301 and hit 41 home runs. He also socked 47 doubles and added 139 runs batted in. The Red Sox won 98 games and a spot in the playoffs.

David hit a game-winning home run to beat the Anaheim Angels in the Division Series. But the Yankees pounded on the Red Sox in the first three games of the ALCS. All seemed lost. No team has ever won a seven-game series after losing the first three games. But then David led them to wins in Games 4 and 5.

Suddenly, the Red Sox were on a roll. The

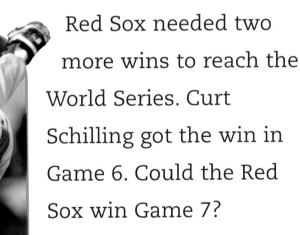

Red Sox needed two more wins to reach the World Series. Curt Schilling got the win in Game 6. Could the Red Sox win Game 7?

Red Sox pitcher Curt Schilling pitched a great game to beat the Yankees in Game 6.

David celebrates with his teammates after beating the Yankees in Game 7 of the ALCS.

In the first inning, David came to the plate with a runner on base. *Bam!* He crushed the ball for a home run! The Red Sox cruised to a 10–3 win. The Red Sox were going to the World Series!

David and his team faced the mighty St. Louis Cardinals. St. Louis had a bunch of super players, including first baseman Albert Pujols, center fielder Jim Edmonds, and third baseman Scott Rolen.

David bashed a home run in his first at-bat in the 2004 World Series.

Game 1 was played at Fenway Park in Boston. David came up to the plate in the first inning. Two Red Sox players were on base. "Papi! Papi!" the crowd chanted. *Boom!* David hit the first pitch he saw high over the wall. The Red Sox had a 3–0 lead! Boston went on to win the game, 11–9. The Red Sox beat up on the Cardinals in the next three games to sweep the series. Boston had won the World Series! David and his teammates celebrated.

The city of Boston exploded with joy. More than one million fans came out to watch the Red Sox victory parade a few days later. David loved every minute of it.

David still crushes the ball for the Red Sox. He keeps practicing and improving. And he has become a fan favorite. In 2005, David was the top vote-getter for the **All-Star Game.**

David celebrates with fans during a huge parade after the Red Sox World Series win.

David finished the 2005 season with his best year yet. He bashed 47 home runs and led the league with 148 runs batted in. No hitter in baseball was more feared than Big Papi. The Red Sox reached the playoffs again. But this time they were knocked out in the first round by the Chicago White Sox.

After many struggles, David is having the time of his life. "I always believed in myself," he said. "What happened to me should teach everybody that you should never give up on anybody."

Young baseball fans really like David. They enjoy his smiling face and happy personality.

Selected Career Highlights

2005 Won Hank Aaron Award for best all-around hitter in the American League
Led the American League with 148 runs batted in
Finished second in the American League with 47 home runs
Finished second in voting for American League Most Valuable Player
Received more fan votes for the All-Star Game than any other player

2004 In 14 playoff games, batted .400 with 5 home runs, 19 runs batted in, and 13 runs scored
Finished fourth in the American League Most Valuable Player (MVP) voting
Named the American League Championship Series MVP
Named the Red Sox Most Valuable Player
Won the Silver Slugger Award for best batting average at his position
Won the Edgar Martinez Award as the league's best designated hitter
Led the American League in extra-base hits
Finished second in the American League with 47 doubles
Finished second in the American League with 41 home runs
Finished second in the American League with 139 runs batted in
Hit a home run in the All-Star Game

2003 Finished fifth in the American League MVP voting
Had a career-high .288 batting average
Hit a major-league-career-high 31 home runs
Earned a major-league-career-high 101 runs batted in

2002 Had a career-best 19-game hitting streak
Helped lead the Twins to the playoffs for the first time since 1991

2001 Had first career two-home run game against the Texas Rangers

2000 Hit first career grand slam against the Boston Red Sox

1999 Playing for the Salt Lake Stingers, led the Pacific Coast League in runs batted in with 110
Named to the AAA All-Star team

1997 Named the Minnesota Twins Minor League Player of the Year

Glossary

All-Star Game: a game played every July in which the best players from each of the major leagues face off

American League Championship Series (ALCS): a series of games played to decide the winner of the American League. The team that wins four games in the series goes on to the World Series.

batting average: a number that describes how often a baseball player makes a base hit

contract: a written agreement between a player and team

designated hitter: a baseball player whose main job is to hit. The designated hitter does not play a position in the field.

Division Series: the first round of the Major League Baseball playoffs

doubles: two-base hits

extra innings: additional innings played if the score is tied after nine innings. Teams play extra innings until one team outscores the other.

free agent: a player who is free to sign with any team

hitting streak: hitting safely in a number of games in a row

home run: a hit that lets the batter circle the bases, cross home plate, and score a run. Home runs are sometimes called homers.

Major League Baseball: The top two professional baseball leagues in North America, the National League and the American League

minor leagues: one of a number of groups of teams in the United States, Canada, Mexico, and Venezuela, where players improve their skills. Most minor league teams are owned by major league clubs.

playoffs: games played to decide which team is the Major League Baseball champion

runs batted in (RBIs): the number of runners able to score on a batter's action, such as a hit or a walk

scouts: in baseball, people who judge the skills of players

spring training: a time from February through March when baseball teams train for the season

World Series: baseball's championship. The winning teams from the National League and American League meet each other in the World Series.

Further Reading & Websites

Buckley, James, Jr. *Play Ball! The Official Major League Baseball Guide for Young Players*. New York: Dorling Kindersley Publishing, Inc., 2002.

____. *The Visual Dictionary of Baseball*. New York, Dorling Kindersley Publishing, Inc., 2001.

Geng, Don. *Play-By-Play Baseball*. Minneapolis: Lerner Publications Company, 2001.

Owens, Thomas S. *Baseball Parks*. Minneapolis: Millbrook Press, 2001.

Boston Red Sox: The Official Site
http://boston.redsox.mlb.com
The official website of the Boston Red Sox includes the team schedule and results, late-breaking news, biographies of past and present players and coaches, and much more.

Major League Baseball: The Official Site
http://mlb.mlb.com
Major League Baseball's official website provides fans with the latest scores and game schedules, as well as information on players, teams, and baseball history.

Sports Illustrated for Kids
http://www.sikids.com
The *Sports Illustrated for Kids* website covers all sports, including baseball.

Index

Photo Acknowledgments

The photographs in this book are reproduced courtesy of: Cindy Loo/
Boston Red Sox, p. 4; © Gary Hershorn/Reuters/CORBIS, p. 5; Julie Cardeiro/
Boston Red Sox, p. 6; AP/Wide World Photos, pp. 7, 9, 15, 17, 19, 22, 25, 28;
Jack Maley/Boston Red Sox, pp. 8, 29; Wisconsin Timber Rattlers, p. 12;
© Darren McCollester/Stringer/Getty Images, p. 14; Minnesota Twins, p. 16;
Chuck Rydlewski/Icon SMI, p. 18; © Mike Segar/Reuters/CORBIS, p. 20;
© Jessica Rinaldi/Reuters/CORBIS, pp. 23, 27; © Rob Tringali/SportsChrome,
p. 24; © Shawn Best/Reuters/CORBIS, p. 26.

Front Cover: © Mike Segar/Reuters/CORBIS